Also by Thomas Devaney

Runaway Goat Cart
Calamity Jane
The Picture that Remains
A Series of Small Boxes
The American Pragmatist Fell in Love
Letters to Ernesto Neto

YOU ARE THE BATTERY Thomas Devaney

ISBN: 978-0-9997028-1-9

BSE Books are distributed by
  Small Press Distribution
  1341 Seventh Street
  Berkeley, CA 94710
  orders@spdbooks.org | www.spdbooks.org | 1-800-869-7553

BSE Books can also be purchased at www.blacksquareeditions.org
and www.hyperallergic.com

Contributions to BSE can be made to
  Off the Park Press, Inc.
  976 Kensington Ave.
  Plainfield, NJ 07060
  (Please make checks payable to Off the Park Press, Inc.)

To contact the Press please write:
  Black Square Editions
  1200 Broadway, Suite 3C
  New York, NY 10001

An independent subsidary of Off the Park Press, Inc.
Member of CLMP.

Publisher: John Yau
Editors: Ronna Lebo and Boni Joi
Design & composition: Shanna Compton

Cover art: *Hiking with You* (2008) by Joy Feasley, vinyl paint on medium density overboard, 30 × 24 inches. Courtesy of the artist.

For Bill Berkson, Marilyn Kane,
and William S. Wilson

Contents

the book of jonah

cold fingers light the way

You Are the Battery

The truth is I follow a miniature pig on social media.

The truth is I actually laughed out loud when I saw the post #EatMoreChicken photoshopped on the side of the pig.

The truth is I don't going around saying things like *the truth is*, not even in a poem.

The truth is I usually take people at their word, even the gods.

The truth is the flowers I received last week made me feel better than anything else.

The truth is, seven years ago I invented an imaginary pig named Bristles.

Bristles kept me busy. Every few days I'd update my lover on all of Bristles's misadventures: the night I saw a cowboy hat inching across the living room floor; Bristles carefully reading *Certain Magical Acts* by Alice Notley (upside down); Bristles in trouble again with Pancetta.

The truth is having an imaginary pig is more work than you might think.

The truth is I'd rather stand-up at the exact moment in the story where I had to stand-up in the story to swoop up to get Bristles back inside, *too close to the balcony ledge!*

The truth is I couldn't stop spinning yarns about Bristles.

The truth is, once you start to saying things like the truth is, it's hard to stop.

The truth is sometimes I think about *the fraction of a fraction of a second* in Olympic games long after the fact.

The truth is I still hate the people who hate me but I now don't care that they hate me.

The truth is I think about my grandmother every day. Her repeaters had a finish, one I remembered recently, "Doctors bury their mistakes."

The truth is batteries are a mix blessing.

The truth is I had a dream I wrote a self-help book called: #You Are the Battery.

The truth is for once I took Allen's advice who told me Bill Burroughs told him to *Get the title first, then write the book.*

The truth I said that the book wrote itself, but it didn't.

The truth is I've forgotten most of what I wrote, but this one sentence: *An appreciation of the cold is a must.*

Brilliant Corners

for Jennie C. Jones

The magic parts before they were burned up and vacuumed.

A sound so light as if no one was there at all.

Your body a buffer between *the same word said at the same time* and other hyper jinx chances.

The dustup made the light look more grey than green.

Time was opened up wider then, so wide in fact that even now it isn't all the way shut.

Horns, sirens, acoustic panels, plenty of *three people can keep a secret, if two are dead* stories to go around.

A late and great string quartet playing in the next room.

I couldn't tell where the music was coming from, and I didn't care.

I was back in high school practicing a clarinet concerto.

And for months, upended by the harp on the headphones in the Chopin waltz.

Walkman freewheeling Sony Walkman—

And only one other person in the world.

                        It does not matter where we fell in, we did.

What she called AC/DC I called AC/DC. Though Monk wasn't Monk, he was MONK: avuncular, like an uncle with no glass in his glasses, poking his fingers *in* to show us.

Not silence, but the stillness of the world; and yet even being still didn't mean you couldn't scratch your nose.

How you once heard the sound of water running under a heavy manhole cover.

The Great Spirit echoing in the old city pipes; the ghost river running under Allegheny Avenue.

Not sound, but the fact of sound.

Not sound or the fact of sound, but the fact of sound after the sound was gone.

Desert Days

1

Prophets say a hard rain, a furious rain—

Or none at all.

A day of destruction and tears.
A day of unprecedented news,
        going bad fast, and *just hell.* But
when the storm came it was a kind of relief.
There was something to do and we did it.

Sandbagging the ocean.

Flocking and lighting a playground of horses on springs red
        yellow blue green crazed orange horses.

Shiny sticker said HERO. That's my brother
        and he is.

JERSEY STRONG, a nice crowd, a good bunch.

2

Even the guy who brags he built his house
　　　　in the middle of the bay, all the other houses
are gone, and yet his house is still standing
　　　　right there—
some feat of engineering and reinforced concrete.
　　　　　　　Wisdom is what you can see.
The views are miraculous. The house is a dream.
We have all we need, thank you for asking.

I dreamt the beach. On the side of the beach.
I mean on the side of a building on the beach.
The building was abandoned, one of those rooms
with water on the floor (a pool?). There was a slide
moving sideways. Out of the corner: a big blue crab
scuttled sideways away with its house on its back.

3

We say electricity and water, risk and beauty. All else
　　　not our problem.

The need for company, the need to be alone: a place on the planet.

One says that she said: "I have a girlfriend. I have a dog. I have a truck.
　　　I live in the desert."

※

I have died many times in my dreams, but on this particular morning,
I had been flying (without a plane) into the desert wind.
　　　　　　　All was open ahead and below
and then in the morning dark, in the living room:
I saw great dunes
　　　on the cover of the Sunday Magazine. My dream,
and the seven-year drought in California, our wars in the desert,
and two bright bowls of sweet potato, turkey tortellini, kale soup.

The dune on the cover was more orange than red, it wasn't Mars,
　　　　　　　　　　but some dried-up sea.
The wilderness was exotic and tempting
　　　　　　　　with a one-word caption: VOYAGES.

　　　Adventure travel,
by the first breath of morning I swallow the Rockies,
the Southwest, Belize, Ecuador, Botswana, Croatia.

Shifts in currency and fortitude. Rugged, right, and worn in,
　　　　　　　　　　our tents are ready.

4

One thing was wanted: a genuine voice.

A red prayer carpet of sound
                to slide down, cling to
                its wall-to-wall weave.

In a downpour the National Guard without music,
the rain conspiring in its own silence.

None of the dogs in the Delta were barking.
Our spirits ceased to brood, but the scent of the wet dog
        stayed on.

5

What we lost when we lost God.

What we lost when we lost the Devil.

What we lost when we had a losing team.

What we lost when we lost the power to lose any of it.

One friend said she broke out in hives—

        face on the carpeted floor
        of the converted basement,
                yet not out.

There were other things we couldn't touch,
        but could touch us:

Look-alike seeds.

Look-alike beaches.

Look-alike islands with a look-alike white man, thumbs up.

Feathers, gold dust, diamonds, and designs—

On Pacific island, ORACLE CEO announced to the locals:
"The Bible says, *Where there is no vision, people perish.*"

6

How much of Chile was gone?
Reports of the 24-hour rainfall in the desert.
Train tracks furiously washed off, and homes totaled,
buried beneath the closed eyes of the heart.
The *Revelations* is a continuous wash of water brown,
turbulent in the face of my neighbor Ramón García Castro.
I saw it, jumping aside from the water as he told me.

Rattled brain said it wasn't responsible for the News.

✳

Had you staked your claim?

At the edge of a continent
                    where the earth surfaces,
a man in a rain jacket and headset:

                    "Let me tell you what you're looking at—
you're looking at power lines. Yes we have lines down.
          Yes we have trees down. Yes we have flooding.
God bless you, godspeed, and good luck."

The ocean was once thought to be bottomless.

There was another idea that it was flat. Now it's invisible.

My uncle told me about the cables that run under the ocean.

The Internet wasn't in the air it was under the ocean.

Cold and immediate dark:

           the gold of old gold medicine

    bottles

lowered   the sweeping countercurrents

            60 feet forward, and 25 back

bright fields flowing from plankton to green   seeded with the sea

          a silvery zone of glycerin and dirt

breath more visible more

     conscious of breathing and the fish there

             are only the eyes of fish

I fix the eyes   put them in front of the heads

         but the eyes are one-sided   long slits

shivering to look at   for too long, the deep places, night swimming

    and friends a quick chill in the nude

             the cables too far down

though cloudy shades of orange glows in a ghost tide of Tide bottles

        sea horses advance into the sound

    of the brain

some deep session   some voluminous bits and morphs absorbed

darting fast *against*   a space tremendous

7

The perfect dinner, setting sun aflame on the Pacific coast—
deep magical, streaming streaks of red

                      during the wildfires the sky itself

        caught on fire.

     That red this foam—

               RED ocean

                 hair

                 feet

                 wine

                 clay

For the earth will grow more stunningly beautiful as it ushers us out.

※

Commentator says, "Look, deserts have always been hotbeds of complaint."
Everyone on the talk show laughs.

One expression of the human heart is to speak the language of sand,
to not so secretly say another way

             to say everything.
Nothing

        was in the clear, and that is OK,
and nothing good was *that* good,

       and that is sad.

             Like soda, why not start with soda?
We drank it and knew all about it,

       but we loved soda, and let it end there.

Air full of vibrations, every ripple in every part of
every other ripple ballooning out of shape.

That day will be a day of a rather remarkable incoherence,
   a day of tropical cyclones and a human chain of ECHO chainsaws,
a day of nine gruesome images and the viral email,
   a day of no balm and "the spill,"
a day of fail-safe procedures and lay it on thick,
   a day of *At least you were not in that* pileup and making it through.

That day will be a day of the full scaled thermal map,
   a day of sleep paralysis and the Great Forgetters,
a day of melting back into rock and leave a bruise—
   a really good bruise. a day of *hold it against m*e,
a day of low visibility and it's all happening—
   a day of haunting beauty and 500,000 spiders in the Missouri bootheel.

No eyes no ears no hands no feet, no thin red line.

The hour of water and air, and rope and bells—
          All ringing all away, the ringing, ringing—
                    the relentless ringing reigning day.

Where in the great glare was I

Under the sun I saw two kids along a long fence
walking   and then fast to a cut, and then we all
were gone. I saw an empty delivery truck with its back
opened as it sped away, twice in the same day.
There was a side field under the sun and I could see
that the grass was wet and dense, with some night still in it.
It had to be freshly cut, but there were no mowers or municipal
ground crews anywhere. A field in my nose, and even now
not a soul to share it.   On the edge of Chinatown an older
couple had just found a bench. They sat closely and looked
straight ahead, one or the other patted the top of the other's hand.

I saw that the secret source of light appear from a brick
pavement stained white at the edges. I saw a splash of little suns
scatter and then restation themselves in the air, light speaking
to light in the eyes of a pair of sunglasses.

Raccoon

I didn't know the strength of
      a city raccoon, which busted out through
my chest, escaped down the side street.
Wild eyes of the raccoon's lightning,
lighting up reflectors
from here to Water Street.
A raccoon uses the full weight of its body
to get what it wants.   Something
in me, some immediate want.
Unburdened by one weight, lit
by another.   Cravings
in the headlights.   On the night
in question, I was a wretch along
railroad tracks, a bulky brown sofa dumped
without its cushions.
Christ and a mouth-thirst,
                all my Jersey devils.

With every trash can lid it flips off
      the raccoon feels more itself.
Prophets and raccoons share
a single ritual: they wash their food.
The row homes sleeping.
The row homes counting their bricks.
        Every night raccoons follow
the same path, they don't go far.
Cellophane wrappers coil in the crabgrass,
dogs down by the river, trails of cinders, piles of

gravel, lines not marked but closely kept.

        Reflectors everywhere: sneakers,
bicycle parts, a STOP sign in a pile of junk in
someone's shared alley space; and rows of painted poles
in the vibrant dark.   Poles of concrete sunk
into the sidewalks so no one can park there.

Background Noise

Children have their own music; and the owls.
The Snow Owl: always five blinks off the beat.
A friend pointing to the eaves at the wildlife preserve:
"This guy's a menace. Barker from a bad circus."
Shake hands with your sister Kate, shake feet with the owls.
City kid, bet your life I was afraid of the owl.
Yes, if you won't bet: still afraid of the owls.

Hour of bottles and breaking glass, not yet day.
Growl of truck, tucked back in, hard to say when
You stopped hearing it. On this particular, Morning says,
The day runs behind the day. Not a dreamsong,
It's true, waiting for Mary. Mary Mary,
      Why all the trucks backing up?
Softly and low toned. Emulation and the owl.

Books on bookcase are taking single breaths.
They want *out.* Like X used to say, such and such
Was under wraps. Honestly, one reason I felt at home
Was I didn't have to keep an eye on my stuff.
Shaped by a half dozen voices, sighs, cries: hear
Tom. Thomas. Tommy Wheels.

Look Me in the Face Sonnet

A side effect of the side effects and a bone-cold day.
The aunt who was more than an aunt came closer
And asked, You alright? Well that's not you.
Not the guy I know. Stop fretting, let's talk. Nobody else
Can tell your story. WHO has that? And me, she said,
What do I want? Look me in the face. OK. I do and
Sit and find out she's been sick for six months.
Why tell? she said. Anyway I'm telling you now:
My body hurts like hell, but my brain is fine.
My appetite is amazing. I'M STILL ME. Do me a favor
And sit for another minute, we don't have to talk so much.
You're hooked with the phone and *the everything else.*
Unplug. Leave it HOME, wherever that is.
When you're doing the dishes: DO the dishes. Tunneling?
Dig the tunnel. Telling a story, tell it to ME.
There's no secret what we need.

Most of Tomorrow

for Bill Berkson

No socks, no Bill, my glasses,

and old No. 2. For the past two weeks on every list

I had his name. "I'll be around most of tomorrow,"

Bill said. And the rest of the time, where? No. 2

added a word or two: annual blood test, *sibling made*

close and breathing throughout, wish I could eavesdrop,

a line disappearing from his mouth   a title, a tune:

Saturday Night. Moon People. Goods and Services.

Repeat after Me. Expect Delays. Portrait and Dream.

Dear Bill. I have a picture of your note in your hand,

it was bruised all over. There's no concealing a hand.

I don't know about that, I can hear him say,

Oh yes you can, oh boy I do, in rich middle tones.

A profile in exile, view over the bay at Cassis.

His friend the journalist from Burgundy, and the cold white

of the white still gives a chill.

Found it back in New Jersey for $120 and considered it.

Now most of tomorrow has been gone for days, yet

the part that was away from the start is still here,

firsthand and near: "Back around 9."

Nine. Nine.   Nine will be fine.

Cold Fingers Light the Way
for Bill Wilson

I read Bill's essay on Ray, it was 100% Bill / 100% Ray.
Walked in the rain and got very soaked.
      The old photocopy had surfaced from a personal slush pile
in the dark lake of the TV room where I had been hiding.
If anyone asked, I would have said I had been following the news.
But it was more than that. I was consumed. I put my stamp on that.

For much of Bill's life he had been in *the New York Correspondence School*:
envelopes, photocopied GUMBALLS FOR SALE, and at least one secret love.

*I will incorporate the letters that seem appropriate in this letter which will be
waiting for you when you return—*

To the end a full head of white hair, stood 6'3" in his stocking feet.
And sharp words for Chelsea and all else that had gone "berserk."

"Scratches show the surface as the surface." More notes scribbled down.

Elsewhere *looking at the views as if I were seeing the feeling I longed to see
and to feel.*   Horses to B, lobsters to A, balloons to K. Twists by the dozens
and turns by the pound.   Bill's limpid prompt to his correspondent to find
the courage to his own tenderness.

An envelope a vehicle of its own. Its indirections home.
Another printed in Sharpie to WILLIAM S. WILSON from RAY JOHNSON
      176 Suffolk Street, New York City, 10002

The letters of each name, a plot as much as they are *instruction for those who would
bury the dead.* Speaking in sweeping monologues to all of the living-room shades.
King Lear of the Chesapeake, standing and gesturing flush in my mind—signing off
in an email: "I cannot draw a cart, nor eat dried oats. If it be man's work, I'll do 't."

To Feel the Minus

Is the wrong way
to put it.
Not that the friend is not here,
the friend is not.
This life, the next
room, pair of good socks,
some click-click up, merry feet,
sativa-lorn scent of geranium,
a name you needn't say to sense.
Why the wise one didn't need to see.
The patch of red
next to identical
is something other than red.
Not as red-faced as the father.
Rosacea is a name to learn
when you are older.
More ghosts
don't mean less lonely.
Colors touch other colors
the answers never come.

A Degree of Intimacy

Remained a rare report.
An impressive lack of symmetry
        conveyed the final evening
of winter, yet winter rallied on a few
months more.
At first blush, cold as our cumbers, we
weighted and good, but then stung in
        the limbs and weeded edges.
How much had our margins of safety betrayed
our hems of distress?
Chanting, not chance. Enchanting, not chance,
        oxygen and espousals.
In time we brightened to the chiming
        likes of "freezingly," or
"cinder blocks."   In our exposure
a stupor of thoughts: "Clear dead blue."
Heat without warmth is the fuck; or
        renouncing the folly of absolute zero:
that somehow our livingest most bits might
                cease all motion.
No, even the frozen world remains a world.
As all poems begin as love poems. Uneven,
bare, future of a better,
        early March always in our ears.
Out we set to the color of ice water as it holds
more names than any day ever could spill.

Mount Hollow Hill

Yards of old cars run over a steep grade,
      nettles and beer caps,
waves of bright and rust up in the hills
      above the valley.
I am somewhere north of Scranton and south
of Carbondale,
      these parts, part of anthracite country,
and the Six Nations before.

A bricked high smokestack without a building
      beneath it.
Lungs, sleek chestnuts, voices in the air—
I keep coming back to what? A few eponymous names
like Pat and Mike, and a mule of a man called Don't mess
      around with Jim. *And with a big drink to you.*
Yeah, you can still hear the *one two three* steam brass
      whistle coming and going.

Across the valley of great aunts and uncles, a voice
      that could only be a grandmother's says,
It's no place for ye. Not for ye or anyone.

Years before I asked if she'd ever heard of
      the Black Irish. "No, Tammy, no."
But then, in another breath said, "Well,
all the Irish were black, black from the mines."

Except this once, my grandmother never spoke of it;
but I remember exactly how her whole forehead tilted

to the back of her head when she said,
"When my father said he'd seen the center of the earth
we could see it in his eyes."

brightest of all subzeros

Several unlit streets ahead

a tugging as if you were prompting yourself to remember the song

it has to be night

that is not optional

it's gone into your body, nothing but night

the final *piano-piano* has been tugged out of you

the whole room in the light

the whole light the whole thing, a dark yet fresh scent

room and mind adjusting   to fade is to remain inside the thought

in the next room screams from a movie, or multiseason series here and gone,
replaced by yourself   your eyes-closed self

minutes and more go by

calm is a state, but the awareness of it puts the calmness in another space inward to
its opened-up breath

as the lightest sounds do dance before sleep and smile from a mile in

that is the feeling, no one else to tell, circle

pools   all can float above them   move free   freely

not circling completely, but a middling muted sound, a sort of widening of yourself,
the whole glow of it, which you carry,   you carry on that way for as long as you can.

Permission to be Crushed

Why I had to leave.

Why I had to walk down certain streets so as not to walk down others.

As soon as you know, you know.

To battle the daemons of my enclave who

give permission every time to smash bottles

against the sewer wall until the feeling passes, or

you run out of Michelobs.

Wide awake in a recent dream, I cannot scale the brick wall.

I can't go over it, and can't go through. I could draw a map,

or make a plan, but why?   That wall is not my wall anymore.

In another dream the next night, a rooting pain

in my right heel.

Extract a vine from the old planter's wart.

It's a muscled vein-root that I can only keep a hold on

with great difficulty, and only with both hands.

Over two feet long, fighting as if to get away.

After, I rub and rub the heel with my thumb.

It's been there all along.

Draw a map, make a plan, whatever you want to call it.

It's taken years to figure out, there's no figuring it out.

The Pileup

At Harvey Fite's place, Ulster County, NY

The sleepy brick smokehouse
tucked away on the dark road, or
the Black Twig apples, they're old
and they're tart, or the grounds-
keeper who pressed the quarry map
with his bloody hand into your own
as you handed him some cash.
Consult the map
      twenty times over-
xeroxed to these softly broken lines.
          Blue stone ramps
and blue stone walkways
that don't lead anywhere,
      worked over for over forty years.
A pool of spiral green,
deep and dead still if you look directly at it.
      I heard the stone here was used
for the Empire State building.
For a long minute, close the eyes,
pan up as fast as you can to the one hundred and two
stories   where the stone and sky meet.
      Here at the far lip of the quarry
stand as close as you can. Another rockshelf
and a cutout section of rubble. Make your way
slowly down to sit. Lean onto your side
and eventually lie down.
Edge to listen   as close you can

the history of the silence of men
quarried and shoveled back in, what's there,
what was made
                    Everything
in the stone yard
                resting on each other.

Concentrate and Continue

There, where the first and last gods kept their tents.

There, where your jaw released a smile.

There, where the good guys didn't win and were not guys.

There, where the page was torn and the morning song continued, nearly unnoticed.

There, where another door would be open to arms reaching for arms that were reaching for them.

There, where the floor did sing, no need to run love aground, the floor did sing.

There, where on getting home from the dance you shut the door and danced each step exactly as it was, curtain to curtain.

There, where you were finally released from the dance.

There, where you had no wallet, but twenty-three singles and some looser change.

There, where in the molecular air, you let the construction sounds wash over you.

There, where *lost sight* walked away from the perpetual pointing of the seeing world.

There, where there would be no need to say something untrue.

There, where your wildest thoughts alighted and you escaped through a pinhole.

Heads Up

I'm keeping my eye on a hawk flying
over 21st and Market.
For all I know the hawk is keeping an eye on me.
     Yesterday the Federal Reserve Bank escaped
being hacked because of a spelling error.
And more events,   but my head is here.
For the moment I can breathe in blue, breathe in green,
breathe out gold.
     A billboard-sized kid running bold in a Blue Cross ad,
baseball glove reaching into the sky "Live Fearlessly."
Trouble afoot and above, you name it. The hawk and me
keeping an eye on that ball and to see who will have
first dibs on the kid.

The Oldest Woman in the World

I didn't read her whole letter right away,
but the first few lines:

    Thank you for sending E and X. . . .

The handwriting in her cursive script, smaller
than anyone else I've ever known,

    and clearer too.

"Tell me your troubles," she'd always said.
And once, that I was an old soul.
From top to toe, scraps of paper smoothed back out.

Creased with a motive and a voice, undimmed
all-the-way-back to 5000 BC

    and other handprints by women.

Did she know the lady Buddha? Socrates?
Of the earth or among the whirling air?
She only said *No, oh no! O those Babylonians!*

The Little Voices of Stillness

It is not the immediate smile, but its softness as it emerges
in my name spoken from under the shadow of a hat.

Scent of angelica, coriander, and juniper berries. Comely sweeps
and unnamed places.

A lingering saline to the taste, plus *buds in March, blossoms in May,*
apples in September.

I surmise that we will get along with the extraterrestrials far better
than we think.

Greetings, alighting, refugees—the city and all of its trees today,
tomorrow, and a long time more.

Memory Corkscrews So You Can't Remember It

I make my prayers in another part of the city,
but they keep blowing back:
      Philly makes, Philly breaks—
What the hell are you looking at?
At the end of the year something
called Sneaker Day,
Swedish Fish and tailpipes in the breeze.
Two kids jamming 2,000-plus Styrofoam cups into
a chain-link fence, spelling out R U N right along
the spillway.

Too young to drive, but opinions carried weight.
The first day of the Cadillac, that first week,
the whole summer, brilliant sunbeads after the rain:
the two-toned Charcoal Caddie.
Jerry Vale came in to get his haircut.

And did they still wear the ponytail style?

Eventually there was a car, a hobbled '74 Pinto,
cheap and easy to park. Driving circles
around one another
      you can run yourself over.
Eating lunch, C said she wouldn't say things
like that, but she wasn't telling me not to,
but maybe don't. I had pizza and a lemonade.

All rumors reset in a blaze over Jersey.

Did the Night Shift and Day Shift ever speak
to each other again?

The year without talking, but music
coming from the little blue car booming inside out—
all the livelong day; a pulse as much as a sound.
      There would be no outside then.
Even the river ran more quietly, the FM radio
streaming more smoothly over the stream.

You almost had to get your ear wet to hear it.

Song of Innocence

it's true, every day really is a new day, as i don't
remember the one before. i get paid in snacks. rice
crispy treats. sour patch kids. chocolate-covered
caramels. my mind and hands have melted into the
sweet life. it's like god in america, take a leap
of faith, or take a seat, you can get the god-thing
right here. i need another job to have a job like this
one. but no one believes in it more than me.

Not a Nice Poem

Fast and polite—
or how about now?
the personal touch
is nice/quaint.
doesn't make much
sense. not helpful,
and more likely to
put you under
suspicion. Why is
so and so being *so* . . .
"Nice guys" who
needs them?
Be nice to yourself,
I'm told, and even that
not said in a nice way.

Ear Tool

Fuck the right fit.
On a ladder
my head hot
near the ceiling
light,
all that working
class crap.
Can hear
the guys
on the jobsite
next door.
The whole
thing
about
the whole
thing, *that*
whole
elbow
brush elbow,
half a nod
short
OK
thing.

I would like to read your Spider-Man poem
a letter to Sparrow

I picture it as a ballet. One without the orchestra.
A solo by Spider-Man occupying the backstage,
up in the upper lightworks. He dips down
      and up again, like two hands playing a piano.
How to explore the vacant vast surrounding?
The shadows are stuttering strobes, so fast
you could not point to a friend to tell him to look
because you know he'd miss it.
Spider-Man was no myth. Yet he trained for other things.
His practice more proportionate and open, than deep
      and simple.

Hell-Dusted Blue Jeans

The Great Plains were overfilled with blue jeans.

During the war, the sky was filled with blue jeans.

Was I making up this story? some voice wanted to know.

Another piped in, *Keep it shut.* The corners of the mouth

in a half half-twist. In high school worked at the Gap

selling jeans, corduroys, Mountain Dew. Provisions of nourishment.

Call of Duty, Mass Effect video games had colonized my

central nervous system. A frame without a mirror to tell me

my fate, I continued a hum along.   Like the Great Depression,

each person blaming him or herself for their own ruin.

The stories are all there.

Sea Breeze Computer

coding Mallarmé

This far inland, eye level
with the driver's seat at shoulder height.
The back seat's influence upon your face.
Again, younger, a game, in *murk mode*,
in *wheeling constellation mode*, a screen,
a bit of a feud, opening to a square of obstacles
repopulating all of them already all
translated, like "Brise Marine,"
and *the scent of the sea*. Spell: *s c e n t*.
Spell: *s e a*. Each more than a tangent to each.
A rare succession! The rain and the fields beyond
feel like magic, and they are. A big fan of the actual
       stuff. A little something for the soul too.
The hill and a two-hundred-year-old doorway,
which for once, you pass right through.

Poem

Today, the first of the year, I write
in concern for my father.
His busted knees, a whole body ache.
His face says more than he does when he says
"I feel better now."

Today, take a walk. Today, call your father.
Sweep the floor.

Shower and wash hair.
Don't turn on TV or go online.
Out my window the vibrations tell me
that two buildings are going up fast.

Today start later, and again. The book
I've been calling *Tell a Story*, or
This Is What I Heard. How to do it, or
say? soaked in and out, all but a watermark.

Today, Jan. 5th, find myself as clear
in my heart as I've ever been, and this too
shall pass.   And say to no one
that I do not mind saying 'I' because
I know that the universe is connected
and this is my portion.

Today, if I knew my own vanity,
how exactly would I tell it? A hidden hand
already tipped?

Today, the thinnest winter branches join in a swath
of pencil-thin plumes.
Keep starting off but getting no nearer to age twelve.
Can't remember a thing, though there are days
I know it wasn't me at all.

Pant leg ripped across the back of the leg,
more close calls   too much sun;
scale   a fence, move along the side of the building
the rooftop, and another curve of a corner.
The soft silver and tar-blackened roof space.
And those pitched black, black windows boxes—
stopping everywhere, beginning
nowhere.

Hungry, again.
I was always hungry.

Near noon, shake it off.
Finally cold, finally January and the year,
if only now   here as much as I ever was.
New enough for something new,
a song, a season—
ice in the river-colored lead,
a pencil number 2.

Today, I write right pass that kid,
the one who I asked to tell me,
          the way he looked right at me,
scar on the chin, and the burn smacked right
across his face.

How to Keep Alive

for M. F. K. Fisher

The Russian River valley in her skinny neck,
And a cordial water.
We never had a chance to meet, but if you need
An aunt my great aunt once said, *get one.*
A slice of nothing is better than nothing.
An open book of *Welcome* and *There Is Nothing Else.*
No stand-in for the fire, but the stove stoked.
As different as any day, and to be in a world
Where the world says *Turn up the fire, yes, now.*
Now is good. And not, *See you in the world.*
Remember favorable November.
And who said that it isn't the meal, but the company?
It is the company, and those Brussels sprout tacos.
The beer is very cold and very brown.

Mount Ephraim by Car

The small rivers in New Jersey
that flow into the nameless.
They're only visible when overrun,
when the creek loses its shape
during storms, or every half mile,
in halfway pauses at the roundabouts.
Teenagers, ring-necked pheasants, and
      engineers know about them,
but it isn't clear how much they
go there anymore.
      By Friday the storm,
or what's left of it will have passed.
      In case we are hungry, in case
we're thirsty—hunger is one instinct,
and a little bit of the dizzy that followed
me into yesterday is another.
Picking up food, two bags of ice,
      and the Pharma ambassador.
The morning I thought,
It wasn't morning and it would never be
      morning.
I used to get lost, though kept a lookout
for the dinosaur on Rt 9, and around the bend,
      the low-graded vista still hits me
like a big mistake.
Passing, passed, to pass—
      Distance is always a dead giveaway that
I'm not looking at what it looks like I am looking at.

When I Felt Free

I did yell.

The light inside: a green
strawberry;
there would be a spring.

I did not question how long
I would feel it,
or ever question if I had: I did.

No one could take that away then,
or ever;
and I could not have said this
then, but the darkness would not end.

Never as free to shine, or sway away,
the whole way away.
A litany of *it got bad fast* stories.

Outnumbered, but your brother stepped out
from the dark, and had a screwdriver by his side.
They backed down. End of that story.

Bad chrome summer bike, why there's
still any space left in those Tues/Weds/Thurs
selfsame days, I do not know.

Nothing lasts, and you were there.

Were you handsome? Could you tell a story?
A good listener?

Brain blocked, LD, or just slow?
Danced in fury.

Was there no shame?
                 Get a name, get a world—
more than five generations worth could name:
Kilroot, Kilkee, Kildare, Kilkenny, Kilmore.
And in light of all that, I say, that on that day
there was no shame.

Not to hear the music, but to have felt song

Whatever the day, or day before that, the feeling
was of sun and grandfather sitting.   Working
my way around the narrow side of the duplex's
backyard. The rhubarb's plumes as tall as me and
the chain-link fence.   And later at the fish hatcheries,
for hours more on end, a crooked concrete chain
of shallow concrete pools, which I can hear.
The warmth on my neck, and no pressure at all.
You and the folding chair were simply there.

One of Those Songs

You haven't heard in a long time.

In the room, air wide open window between

you and everything. This one 99 Red Balloons,

but in German, 99 Luftballons.

The drums and bass synth *locked in* that driving beat.

A song speaking the Nerf-edged innocence Pop sound

in any pop language. *Ich spreche ein bisschen.*

The scent of mouse in the hair of the world

I was born into.   And if it's in the air

and you know how to breathe, you won't know

what isn't possible.   And what's more in store

for a day traded in for a mile-long smile?

Who has her license? Who can drive?

Cars and people in other countries go faster.

The sweet rips the clear right open.

Brightest of All Subzeros

Eyes closed don't mean we're dead.
The young can love each other,
as they do, and it's weird, as they say,
and they know it.
But we are not them; and being born
never gets any easier.
Pressure per square inch: a half-built igloo,
no roof so we can take in as much of the snow
as can be taken in—
In the pitch of its drifts running off without us,
this open, blinding field hides as much as it shows.
It isn't the love of love that we love, but the winter light.
Angle out as wide as you can to get the shot.

Journal Entries

I said I could take or leave my own words as
a background check, which would find me out
much later: the world-as-book, more real than myself.
There's a line in Ron Padgett's "Reading Reverdy"
where *the line part of yourself goes out to infinity*.
I say you can take or leave those words, something
          cut loose in the comment, except
there's another thing, an echo in another notebook,
a finger-printed phrase that's never left my head—
Let go Let go / Let / Really go.

Dark day flies away

for Joanne Kyger

This day
I said   *I'd resist*
softly
        but a pencil
pressing
as much as it needs to be

Afternoon was half hiding
        How to listen to the winter
light
        peeking through

It must have been 4:30 or 5 o'clock
at a makeshift kitchen counter
        from dark side of the warehouse
up across the other side
darker still
a bird too small and too fast to name
a vision twenty-two years ago
here, now
so much
like
    light

The Thing I Must Tell You

after a recording of Wisława Szymborska

Like a stone thrown straight into the river.
The eyes, the face and eyes. The urgency
to see the only eyes that those eyes must see.

They're hazel and do not flinch.
They say: *Yes, Right,* or *No.*
> *They're licked.* Or:
Like running across the Boulevard,
hand holding an arm, or another hand,
tomorrow
> and now.
Rye bread, vodka, and a canvas bag.
> Late in the day,
everyone's favorite Aunt Peg cuts to the quick
in Port Richman; and Jimmy "the Mayor"
Lemanowicz WILL BE BACK TOMORROW,
or so says a sign on the river wards.
A lip of light on the head shining ahead.
It's never not late. And again:
Jak kamień rzucony do wody.
It's me or not me I overheard the Baba say
> to her Alan, Alan.
Held, not in a gentleness,
> but in the pitch black quiet of her coat.
There, there was nobody else. No horde in that space
that could push us out.

Jerome, Jerome

after hearing Jerome Kizke

Tall stride and his gait: the whole
long-haired history
and an enameled flame, my own
version of him,
      and his name said once.

That which makes the inner ear hear
but is harder to hear.
The way a name comes to sound like itself.

That he called me by my full name too.

Snow fields down the dirt road.
There was a field down that minivan road,
we met there.

Drum   *ear drum*
         ear drum   *drum.*

Splayed pink knuckles and a keening wish,
     the whole thing
     his own name
     said   as many times as any
that you've ever said as much.

And maybe we still didn't know how to say
each other.

And may we never do, and never be afraid not to.

Fitting the Bill

Giveaways include: full names, pointed disagreements, allowing
the host of the party to cut your hair. Was it ever a question
that *so and so* was gay? and that you were *they*? No passport.
Two blackbirds on the wall made visible by the photograph and
the shadow of the trees coming out of your head. You took intrigue
off the table a while ago, and so it continued. You learned or
simply figured out how not to show your hand, but also how not to
hold back "physically." What looked one way as you spoke, felt
another as you heard yourself say: *one tablespoon Dijon, one miso,
lemon juice, lemon zest* (and parmesan?). Rain: IN. Rain checks: OUT.
Despite names that do or do not exactly fit, despite a cello/tabla combo,
a pang a good hair ahead of the beat: first mothlike against the wall, then
spinning in the dark, no one giving anything away. Not a thing.

The Last Ones

Who was the last one to hate the last snowfall?

There was no visibility out of the side of the eyes,
yet you pushed on as well as you could, each step
        as much *in place* as it was ahead.
If you ever made it home there would be two or three
ailing plants, and that would not be so bad
for a few months away.

A window opened now and it's chilly.
There are things that tell you that you should
keep it shut, but you don't
as you need the fix—
         an untrammeled field of snow
stuck in the front part of your head,
as shocking as any in the *Revelations*.

You can't smell the pine, but that's OK.
Way out in the field   you and the gashed tree,
the one you called the Opera. Its body burnt through
by lightning, and its lone bough outstretched, hit
so many times. Its violence, its silence, out in the open.

The tree turns in your trudge, so many lives,
and higher up as if proud, pass the swell
        and passed the plowed road—
Clump of snowdrops in the snow. *Snow feed me snow.*
How many more blocks are there left to go?

Untitled

And then you understood there would be no more life of music.

And then you understood touching your temple on a bus that you would grow old there, or on a train for yourself and another.

And then in a whole other life you understood you could not be on the same coast without knowing it, and you could not be on the same coast.

And then you understood not to tell jokes to strangers.

And then you understood the shameful sound of *wood* in water.

And then you understood the spot on the ground where nothing grew.

And then you understood that the skyline comes from a whole other world.

And then you understood you were a white man. Whatever else you felt about yourself. You were that.

And then you understood why you made the long trip to sit at a table closely reading a book with others. A witness to *hevel* and yourself.

And then you understood it was not about understanding.

And then you understood we would not be friends, and that would have to be OK.

the book of jonah

The Thread

Right, looking is not enough,
and the voice that pops up
to say it isn't enough
isn't either.   All things
from the very first,
unlike anything else.
The brain and body
don't always partner, and
are quick to call
          each other out
and even fools. Yet the road isn't
blocked by the sphinx.
The riddle we were told was
a front story, the one not spoken
is still very much around.

The Prehistory of March

Don't say scrapes, or nylon stitches
Say blood and the light in a glass of water
Say you're playing a game of wireball with gravity
Say you're not keeping score, but falling behind
Say ready or not
Say the lack of eye contact, or not even looking
Say he's slow, the turtle, little shit, *you're it*
Say this line is blank
Say it will take years
Say it will take longer than that
Say the day and night will be your witness
Say you will be your own proof
Say it's the time before the time to sleep
Say the dream can be wakeful
Say the days are not done, though some will be dusted
Say the cold will still be cold
Say the words *all* and *together* together
Say if no contact now, then a rendezvous
Say the hard bones have yet to be born
Say that somewhere there is a room
Say you are in that room right now

A Body in a Room

1

A body covered in dust in a room covered in dust.

A body its existence, dark spot on the ground.

A room admitted to itself.

A body that had studied a room like a book.

A room on its cold knees.

A body surrendering to itself by degrees.

A room blanketed, a body folded over.

A room of unmeasured breaths.

A room with no inkling of what a body will do next.

A body as it tortoised-and-hared its way through a room.

A body running a fever.

A body, a room. *Who's in there?*

A body breaking off a thought, a gasp.

A room a body was *done in* in, a mystery.

A room a breach, a body gone to flowers.

2

A room and a body and the music they liked.

A body repeating itself *peanut knows knows knows, peanut knows.*

A body coursing and room refraining. *A room a room—*

A room many rooms ago, a skipping record.

A body a pretty serious metronome.

A room a well of dark. The day's crazy not yet departed.

A body that shared a password with a room, they were that close.

A room a good friend to at least three people, maybe four.

A body and its ugly knees.

A room that could answer as easily as sneeze.

A room a dimmer switch for a body.

A room and its sex, a body and its sexes.

A body and a room, necking and neck.

A body as it rifled through a room for a piece of paper.

A body holding out, a room with no EXIT sign.

3

A room a stranger at first, the light low.

A room dense with plant life. Neither the forest, nor the far back fields, but a little bit of both.

A body that died for truth, a room that died for beauty.

A room that grew into its proverbial posters.

A body *whose face gives no light, shall never become a star.*

A body its first Bonnie, a room shy, high, exalted.

A room where you can be where you've never been before.

A room that had no way of being framed.

A room a sound of soon.

A body, a brief history of light in a room.

A room called *bastard* and its vagrant heart.

A body a star westward from the pole, a room illuminated where it burned.

A body of the east that was green, black body of the north, red body of the south, white body of the west, a room for each.

A room released from any sense of intelligibility.

A room without corners, a body yielding to the earth of its dreams.

The Book of Jonah

Did he get on the first ship he could find that was going out?

From what was he running?

If you wished to fall off the face of the earth, is there a better place to stow away than in a ship destined for Tarshish?

And why ask if the great wind sent into the sea was sent by God?

What about waking nightmares, how do you wake from those?

Was the great fish really a whale? Either way, is it surprising that such leviathans haunt the imagination?

Was there ever a moment in the belly without terror? Could there be some private joy?

How is it in your own stomach? Your chest?

Where does a cry from such a place go?

What if those prayers were actually heard?

Who can say what power is held in that?

Why does the specter of a pointed finger rarely fade?

"Even to the soul." If it was a question could it be one for long?

When the great fish spits him out at the Lord's command, isn't there a gap in the story there?

For isn't the racking release into the waterwheel as considerable as the oblivion spent in the belly of the whale?

And just how deep do the conventions of the horror story go into the psyche?

What could be more inventive than the mind of an addict, an improvised allegory?

Was this but another elaborate yarn spun by a junkie?

What is the space between the voice of thanks and true thanksgiving?

And when others believe you more than you believe yourself, isn't that its own special kind of hell?

To what degree do *they that observe lying vanities forsake their own mercy*?

But if you didn't feel that you weren't feeling it, was it possible that affecting gratitude was not exactly a lie?

How much patience does even a patient god have to have?

Do people change?

Yet didn't he convey that *kingdom come* was coming as he was commanded?

How is it that you could convince a city of its own doom and still be hustling yourself?

How is it that you could ask people of a great city to mend their ways, and yet when they do, you're still AWOL to yourself?

Is this what anger which is greater than fear looks like?

When you did everything you could to *do yourself in* and yet still didn't go, was that the sign to beseech the Lord to end it right there?

What about the plank pushed down over your chest so hard that you didn't know it was there at all?

Is this how the body speaks itself past words?

The night Jonah found himself sitting outside on a blanket and beheld that it was he himself who was sitting. Was this the first time there was no question?

Did his name really mean dove?

Did building the makeshift shed give as much satisfaction as the shelter it provided?

In pencil drawings of apples have you ever detected a skull?

And what of the gourd?

Did the worm that would soon wither the gourd really take anything away from the first gladness of its shape?

Was it true that anyone had to focus on the vehement east wind just because it was coming?

Could the question *is there such a thing as silence* ever be asked again?

Acknowledgments

This book is dedicated to Bill Berkson (1939–2016), Marylin Kane (1936–2016), and Bill (William S.) Wilson (1932–2016): friends, teachers, torchbearers. They all died within a few months of each other. Talking with Bill Berkson was one of the great pleasures of my life. Seek out Bill's voice in our conversation, "The kind of story that music is" in the *Brooklyn Rail* Nov. 2017. | Marilyn Kane was a nun for thirty years in the Sisters of the Holy Names of Jesus and Mary. She left the convent and moved to San Francisco. She met poet Carl Rakosi who was in his mid-eighties at the time and died in 2004 at 101 years old. For fifteen years they had a great love. George Albon calls Marylin the female Candide. "Look Me in the Fact Sonnet" was written for Kane. | In 1999, Bill Wilson wrote me a letter after reading my first book *The American Pragmatist Fell in Love*. He picked it up in David Reed's studio where my close friend Dean Daderko was working. Wilson and I grew to be friends and remained in correspondence until his death. The line "instruction for those who would bury the dead," in my poem "Cold Fingers," is by my teacher and friend Louis Askeoff, from his book *Freedom Hill*, which is also dedicated to Wilson.

A number of the poems in the collection grew out of a Midrash workshop with Alicia Ostriker between 2014-2017.

Thanks to Elizabeth Savage, Jay Kirk, Cynthia Arrieu-King, Eleanor Wilner, Cort Day, Trevor Winkfield, Gaelen Hanson, Laura McGrane, Olivia Haber-Greenwood, Natasha Cohen-Carroll, John Emil Vincent, Delia Bowman, and Jonathan Rabinowitz (for introducing me to Herbert Morris's *The Little Voices of the Pears*). The book was completed in part during a Pew Fellowship in the Arts, which included residencies at the MacDowell Colony and the Banff Centre. Special thanks to Melissa Franklin for her support, to Joy Feasley for her artwork, and to Shanna Compton for the book design. Thanks and much love to Amy Sadao and to my parents, Maureen and Tom. Great thanks to John Yau and Black Square Editions.

Grateful acknowledge is due to the editors of the following journals and online magazines in which these poems first appeared:

Best American Poetry 2019, "Brilliant Corners."

Palette Poetry, May 2018, "A Body in a Room."

The American Poetry Review, January/February 2018: "Where in the great glare was I," "Raccoon," and "The Book of Jonah."

The Brooklyn Rail, January 2018: "Brilliant Corners," "Cold Fingers Light the Way," "Hell-Dusted Blue Jeans," "Most of Tomorrow," "Memory Corkscrews So You Can't Remember It."

Kestrel issue 35, fall 2016: "The Thing I Must Tell You."

Bedfellows Magazine 5, spring 2016: "Brightest of All Subzeros."

"Poetic Address to the Nation," Painted Bride Arts Center Philadelphia, February 2016: "Look Me in the Face Sonnet." Also published in *Cruel Garters*, 2019.

The AWL, Dec 10, 2015: a variant of "Background Noise."

Sea Change, catalogue for Zoe Strauss's show at Cantor Fitzgerald Gallery, Haverford College, January 2015: "Desert Days." The show traced the effects of climate change in America.

About the Author

Thomas Devaney is the author of *Runaway Goat Cart, The Picture that Remains* (with the photographer Will Brown), *A Series of Small Boxes, The American Pragmatist Fell in Love,* and the solo-opera *Calamity Jane.* He is a 2014 Pew Fellow. He lives in Philadelphia and currently teaches at Haverford College.